THE D.I.Y. JOKE BOOK

belongs to

_____

The
D.I.Y. Joke Book

Peter Eldin

Illustrated by Alan Rowe

BEAVER BOOKS

A Beaver Book
Published by Arrow Books Limited
62–5 Chandos Place, London WC2N 4NW

An imprint of Century Hutchinson Ltd

London Melbourne Sydney Auckland
Johannesburg and agencies throughout the world

First published 1989

Set in Century Schoolbook
by JH Graphics Ltd, Reading

Printed and bound in Great Britain by
Anchor Press Ltd, Tiptree, Essex

ISBN 0 09 964560 2

Contents

Introduction

D.I.Y? Do It Yourself, of course! But this is not a Do-It-Yourself book in the accepted sense for it will not tell you how to make a set of book shelves or lay a patio.

And, although the title *The D.I.Y. Joke Book* may give the impression that it is a joke book, it is also an unusual quiz book.

If you like jokes, this is the book for you. And if you like quizzes, this is the book for you. Even if you do not like quizzes, this is the book for you for in several of the quizzes there are no correct or incorrect answers and you can make them up as you please.

Why have quizzes for which there are no absolutely correct answers? The reason is that they are designed to get you thinking about jokes and how they are formed. And it should not be long before you are making up jokes of your own.

At some time or another all of us have said or written something we thought was funny. Now *The D.I.Y. Joke Book* will help every aspiring comedian to write his or her own jokes — and have fun at the same time.

Variations on a Theme

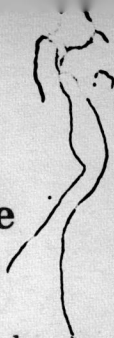

The easiest way to make up your own jokes is simply to vary some of the jokes you know already. If you think about certain jokes you will almost always come up with some new ideas.

Try changing the last line of a simple joke. Take the old chestnut, 'Why did the chicken cross the road?', the answer to which is usually 'To get to the other side'. How can we change the last line to come up with a different joke?

Let's try:

Why did the chicken cross the road?

> *For some fowl purpose.*
> *Someone egged her on.*
> *She was looking for her mother and feather.*

Well, there's three different answers (and, therefore, three different jokes) for a start.

If you cannot come up with answers straight away try thinking of words associated with your subject and this may spark off a few ideas. The word 'chicken' may bring to mind 'fowl', 'egg', 'feather' (and that's how the answers given above came into being). Other words might be 'nest', 'rooster, 'hen'.

Here are some more ideas:

Why did the chicken cross the road?

Because she saw the zebra crossing.
For fun and hen-tertainment.
Because she was tired of being cooped up.
Because she saw a man laying bricks and wanted to know how to do it.

Well, that's quite enough variations on that joke for the moment. You'll find some more later in the book but, in the meantime, try doing the same thing with other jokes you know. It can be great fun — and you may even come up with some new jokes to amuse your family and friends.

Finish 'Em Off

The jokes in this section do not have any tag lines. See if you can devise a final laugh line for each joke.

Some possible answers are given on page 119 but you may think of something different for there are no right or wrong answers. Whatever you think is apt and amusing will probably do just as well.

1 What did the little apple say to the big apple?

2 What's the best thing for water on the knee?

3 What did the carpet say to the floor?

4 What is a cat's favourite holiday resort?

5 What is a duck's favourite television programme?

6 What is the best thing to do when your car brakes don't work?

7 Why did the cow jump over the moon?

8 What did the big flower say to the little flower?

9 What runs but cannot walk?

10 Where do pigs go on their holidays?

11 If you get umpires in cricket and referees in football, what do you get in bowls?

12 Why do witches fly on broomsticks?

I Wouldn't Say . . .

Several alternative tag lines are given for each of the following remarks. See if you can think of any more.

I wouldn't say my mum is fat but . . .

   . . . Dad takes a walk around her when he wants exercise.

   . . . she can sit round the table all by herself.

   . . . every time she falls down she rocks herself to sleep trying to get up.

   . . . when she gets off a bus five people can get on.

   . . . she can take a shower without getting her feet wet.

   . . . Dad has to kneel up in bed to see if it's daylight.

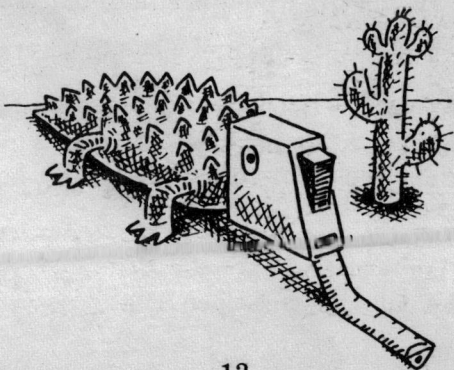

I wouldn't say my friend is skinny but . . .

> . . . we use him as a bookmark.
> . . . his father uses him as a pipe cleaner.
> . . . he doesn't even cast a shadow.
> . . . he can hide behind a flag pole.
> . . . his mother keeps him in the spaghetti jar.

I wouldn't say my mum's a bad cook but . . .

> . . . Dad always puts an altar cloth on the table because he's been served so many burnt offerings.
> . . . pygmies come from Africa to dip their arrow heads in her stew.
> . . . have one of her meals and you'll never live to regret it.
> . . . we always say a prayer before we have lunch.
> . . . our dustbin has ulcers.
> . . . have you ever tried eating gravy with a knife and fork?
> . . . she tried to bake a birthday cake but the candles melted in the oven.

I'm not saying my friend is stupid but . . .

> . . . she sits at the back of a bus to get a longer ride.
> . . . she buried her car battery because the mechanic said it was dead.
> . . . when she went to a mind-reader he only charged her half price.
> . . . if she wants to count to twenty she has to take her socks off.
> . . . she calls her pet tiger Spot.

14

. . . she's been learning to play the violin for ten years and she's only just discovered that you don't blow it.

. . . she put 'wool' labels in all her clothes to fool the moths.
. . . she once got off her bike when someone told her that the wheels were tyred.

I wouldn't say my sister is shy but . . .

. . . she goes into another room to change her mind.
. . . she blindfolds herself when she takes a bath.
. . . she was born wearing a nappy.
. . . she covers the bird-cage every time she undresses.

I wouldn't say Fred Idle was lazy but . . .

. . . when he drops something he waits until he has to tie his shoe laces before he'll pick it up.
. . . he gets tired brushing his teeth.

I wouldn't say I'm unlucky but . . .

. . . aspirins give me a headache.
. . . I once had an artificial flower that died.
. . . when I return in the next life I shall probably be a centipede with ingrowing toenails.
. . . you've heard of feet that go to sleep? Mine snore!

I wouldn't say my sister was conceited but . . .

. . . she has a mirror on the ceiling so she can watch herself gargle.
. . . she is always me-deep in conversation.
. . . when she hears a clap of thunder she goes to the window and takes a bow.

Let's Change the Subject

One way to alter jokes you find is to change the subject of the joke.

Take a joke and see how many variations you can get from it.

For example:

How can you tell if an elephant has been in your fridge?

There are footprints in the butter.

Change the word 'elephant' to 'philatelist' (stamp collector) and you could come up with the joke:

How can you tell if a philatelist has been in your fridge?

He's stamped all over the butter.

Here are some other ideas. See if you can come up with any more.

How can you tell if a glutton has been in your fridge?
There's nothing left.

How can you tell if a dentist has been in your fridge?
There are teeth marks in the cheese.

How can you tell if a vampire has been in your fridge?
All the blood oranges have gone.

Let us take another look at the old 'Why did the chicken cross the road?' which we altered earlier by changing the last line. Using the 'change the subject' idea you can try using other creatures instead of the chicken and see what you can come up with.

Here are some examples:

Why did the rooster cross the road?
To show he wasn't chicken.

Why did the hedgehog cross the road?
To see his flat mate!

Why did the blind chicken cross the road?
To go to the Bird's Eye shop.

Why did the Manx cat cross the road?
To go to the re-tailer.

Why did the one-armed man cross the road?
To visit the second-hand shop.

Why did the tortoise cross the road?
To go to the Shell garage.

Why did the elephant cross the road?
He wanted to make a trunk call.

Sometimes you will find that trying a substitute may not work but on occasions it will help you to think up a completely new joke.

What Is the Question?

If someone tells you the last line of a two-line joke can you work out what the first line should be? Here are some tag lines; what was the question posed in each case?

If you have no idea turn to page 120 for the answers, I mean questions.

If you have no idea turn to page 120 for the answers, I mean questions.

1 *The collie wobbles.*

2 *Mary Christmas.*

3 *He wanted to draw the curtains.*

4 *Don't look now, I'm changing.*

5 *Don't blame me. I only laid the table.*

6 *Just tell me where the pane is.*

7 *A navvylanche.*

8 *Apple grumble.*

9 *Ruff.*

10 *Grandma.*

11 *The can-can.*

12 *Yes, no, yes, no, yes, no . . .*

13 *Sixteen. Four richer, four poorer, four better, four worse.*

14 *He wanted to lie low for a while.*

15 *A basketball.*

16 *One was made of wood, the other was Maid of
Orleans.*

General Knowledge Quiz

Here is a quiz to test your general knowledge –
but be careful, the answers may not be quite so
straightforward as they appear.

You will find the answers on page 120.

1 Where was Solomon's temple?

2 What book teaches you how to fight?

3 What car is popular in China?

4 What do Eskimos use for money?

5 What is a metronome?

6 Why did the Romans build straight roads?

7 What is an autobiography?

8 Why do glow worms glow?

9 What is a biplane?

10 How does an Eskimo make a house from blocks
of ice?

11 Which Middle Eastern person invented
flavoured crisps?

12 How do you make a cannonball?

13 What do you call a judge with no fingers?

14 How would you cut the material for a Roman toga?

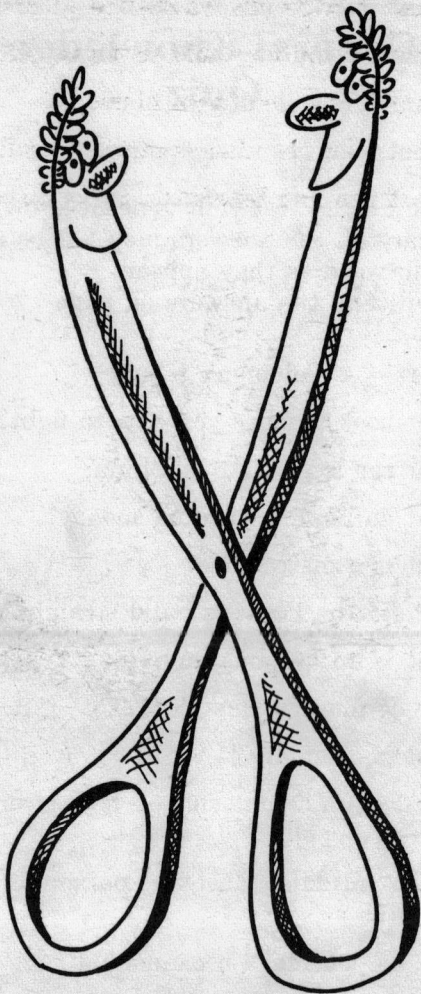

15 What do you give to someone who has everything?

16 What word is always spelled incorrectly?

17 What do you buy only to throw out?

18 What fills a field with music?

19 What men are always above board?

20 What can you break by saying it?

Find the Words

In this section each joke has one or more words missing. Can you work out what the missing words should be. Some possible answers are listed on page 121.

1 What do you get when you pour _____ _____ down a rabbit hole?
Hot cross bunnies.

2 Waiter, what's this _____ doing in my soup?
The breast stroke, I think, sir.

3 GARDENER: I put _____ on my rhubarb.
BOY: *Really? I always put custard on mine.*

4 What is a _____ ?
A female moth.

5 What happened to the man who didn't know the difference between _____ and putty?
His windows fell out.

6 What would you get if you crossed a blizzard with a _____
Frostbite.

7 What do you get if you cross a _____ with a dog?
Very nervous postmen.

8 What did one _____ say to the other?
I'm going out tonight.

9 What would you get if you piled lots of _____ on top of each other?
The leaning tower of pizza.

10 What's the difference between a _____ and a bully?
You lick one, the other licks you.

11 Do you think I could borrow your _____?
Certainly . . . provided you don't take it out of my garden.

12 What can you step in when it is raining
_____ _____ _____ ?

Poodles.

All Change

In earlier sections we saw how a new joke can be made from an old one by altering the last line or by changing the subject. By using both of these methods together you can come up with even more jokes. Yes, we are back to that chicken crossing the road again!

Here we go:

Why did the chicken cross the railway track?
Because she wanted to lay it on the line.

Why did the chicken stand in the middle of the road?
Because she was a Rhode Island.

Why did the germ cross the microscope?
  To get to the other slide.

Why did the sailor cross the ocean?
Because he wanted to get to the other tide.

And that is enough of that particular joke! Let's look at some other jokes and how they can be varied:

What has four legs and flies?
A dead horse.

What has two legs and flies?
A pair of trousers.

What has wellies and flies?
A fisherman.

What has boy scouts and flies?
A tent.

What is green, has lots of teeth and looks like a street.
An alleygator.

What is green, has lots of teeth and holds up your socks?
An alligarter.

What is green, has lots of teeth and goes to see the doctor?
An illigator.

What is green, crispy and religious?
Lettuce pray.

What is green, crispy and difficult to understand?
Lettuce think about it.

What is in honeymoon salad?
Lettuce alone.

What do you give a bruised lemon?
  Lemon aid.

What do you call a cat that works in a hospital?
  A first-aid kit.

What do you give a man who hasn't had a drink for three days?

Thirst aid.

What do you give a busted balloon?

Burst aid.

What is administered by a quick ambulance man?

Fast aid.

What is administered by an incompetent doctor?

Worst aid.

What type of carpet would you find at the United Nations?

A diplo-mat.

What type of friend would you have at the United Nations?

A diplo-mate.

What type of dog would you find at the United Nations?

A diplo-mutt.

What type of crazy person would you find at the United Nations?

A diplo-nut.

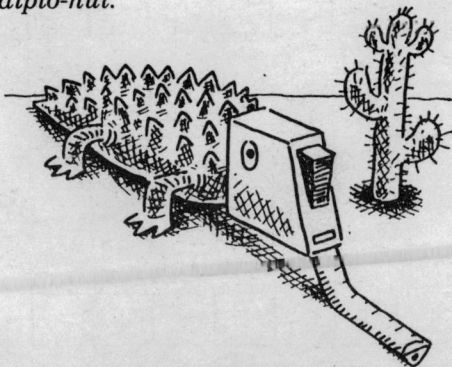

Jokes to Fit

The answers to each of the jokes in this section fit into the grid shown.

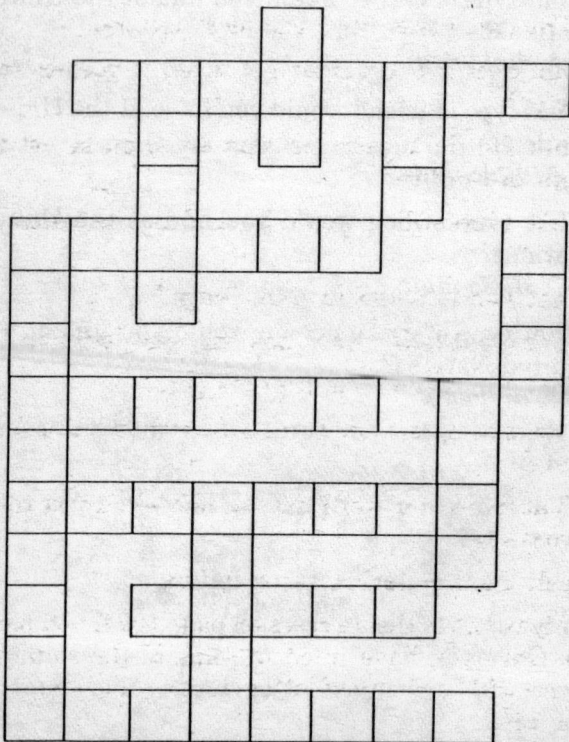

Can you use your ready wit to work out what each answer should be and then apply your fantastic brain power to put the words into the squares?

What is the most important school subject for a witch?

What do you do when your nose goes on strike?

It comes with an aeroplane, is of no use to the aeroplane but the aeroplane never goes without it. What is it?

What two words have the most letters?

What does a budgerigar get when it goes to the doctor?

What did the plastic surgeon do when he sat in front of the fire?

What plays when it works and works when it plays?

What fish is found in a bird-cage?

What eight-letter word has only one letter in it?

What illness do retired pilots get?

If two's company and three's a crowd, what is four and five?

What five-letter word has six left when you take two away?

Spell 'hard water' in three letters.

Only resort to the answers on page 122 if you have to. Once you have filled in some of the squares, there will be plenty of letter clues to help you with the rest.

Daft Definitions

A popular type of joke is the daft definition. To test ability with jokes and words try this quiz. All the words listed here have been defined below. See if you can work out which word belongs to each definition. Don't forget that this is a joke book so the definitions may not be exactly what you would find in an ordinary dictionary.

The answers are given on page 122.

1 Hatchet. 2 Advice. 3 Cannibal. 4 Dogma. 5 Barbecue. 6 Buttress. 7 Mistake. 8 Aperitif. 9 Illegal. 10 Coward. 11 Drip. 12 Parent.

a) A pair of dentures.
b) Line up a hairdresser's.
c) A sick bird.
d) What a bird tries to do when it sits on an egg.
e) A man who wears water-wings in his bath.
f) A person who sleeps when the baby isn't looking.
g) A man who has friends for dinner.
h) The mother of pups.
i) Something which everyone gives but few people take.
j) Someone you can always hear but can never turn off.
k) A woman shoplifter.
l) A female goat.

Crazy Mixed-up Jokes

The tag line for each of the jokes in this section answers one of the other joke questions. Can you work out where each tag line belongs? See page 122 for the answers, if you have no idea or are too lazy to think about it!

1 What do you call a frog spy?
   a) *Toot-and-come-in.*

2 Where do German cars go when they get old?
   b) *Double Dutch.*

3 What makes the Tower of Pisa lean?
   c) *A leg.*

4 What do twins in Holland speak?
   d) *A porcupine.*

5 How did Vikings communicate?
  e) *A bad golfer.*

6 What do you get if you cross a citrus fruit with a bell?
  f) *The old Volks home.*

7 What notice is under an Egyptian doorbell?
  g) *A strict diet.*

8 What goes putt, putt, putt?
  h) *An orange that can peal itself.*

9 What carries lots of needles but never does any sewing?
  i) *They used the Norse code.*

10 What has a bottom at its top?
  j) *A croak and dagger agent.*

Birds of a Feather

The answer to each of these jokes is a bird of some sort. Given that clue, can you work out the answers? If you can't you will find them on page 123.

1 What bird cannot fly away?

2 What bird is present when you have a meal?

3 What bird can carry heavy weights?

4 What pie can fly?

5 What do you use to unlock a Turkish house?

6 What bird is covered in chocolate?

7 What bird is musical?

8 What bird is always miserable?

9 What bird is always out of breath?

10 What bird is made of paper and tied to a string?

11 What bird is a bit of fun?

12 What flies and is a crime?

Personalizing Jokes

To give your jokes more impact when you tell them it is often a good idea to put a specific name to a character in a joke. This makes it much more interesting to the people listening.

So if a joke starts 'A man went into a pub . . .' it will be much more effective if you say, 'My uncle Bob (or whatever your uncle's name happens to be) . . .'

This idea can be extended to places and street names. So instead of saying, 'A man walked down a street . . .' change it to someone you know walking down a street you know. 'A man walked down a street' is fairly ordinary, but if you say Fred Bloggs (or someone you and your listeners know about) was walking along Beehive Lane (a local street) it becomes much more interesting.

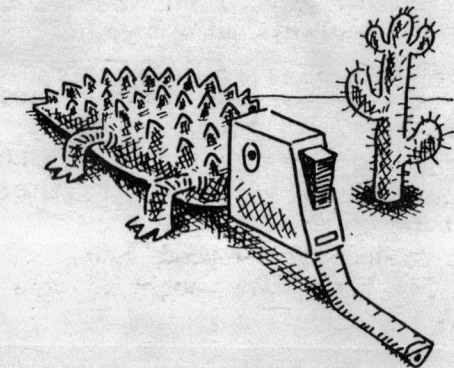

But be careful when using this technique. Only use it if the joke is harmless and will not upset anyone. You could get yourself into trouble if your friends believe that what you are saying is true!

Here are some jokes in which you could insert names and places you know to make them more interesting:

_____ (name of local shop) are now selling television sets with a year's guarantee. That means, if the set breaks down they guarantee it will be a year before they come to fix it.

Mrs _____ (name of neighbour) woke her husband up the other night and said, _____' (husband's name), I've just been downstairs and there's a burglar in the kitchen eating my freshly made fruit cake! Ring 999!'

'Who should I ask for?' said _____ (husband's name). 'Police or ambulance?'

Mr _____ (someone you know) was driving along _____ (local road) when, to his amazement, he was overtaken by _____ (friend's name) riding a bicycle.

He picked up speed but a short while later _____ (friend) passed him again, pedalling like mad.

This happened a few more times and eventually Mr _____ (you know who) stopped the car to see what was going on.

'Thank goodness you stopped,' said _____ (friend). 'My braces are caught in your rear bumper.'

Did you hear about _____ _____ (friend's name) the other day?

He went into _____ (local clothes shop) and said, 'Can I try that suit on in the window?'

The manager replied, 'No, sir. You'll have to try it on in the changing room like everyone else.'

The other day Mrs _____ (friend of the
family) went into _____ (local hardware shop)
and asked for something to help with her spring
cleaning.

'I've just the thing,' said the salesman.

'This wonder polish will do half the job for you.'

'In that case,' said Mrs _____ (whatever
her name is), 'I'll take two tins.'

Mrs _____ (neighbour) went into _____
(local shoe repair shop) yesterday and said, 'I want
these shoes soled by tomorrow morning.'

She went back this morning and asked about the
shoes. The assistant gave her £2.50.

'What's this for?' asked Mrs _____ (what's-
her-name).

'It's for the shoes,' the assistant replied. 'I sold
them as you asked.'

Who's There?

'Knock, knock' stories make good jokes when personalized, as described in the last chapter.

To do this write down the name of a friend (if you still have any after cracking lots of jokes about them). Now write down as many words or phrases that sound like the name as you can.

Let's take an example: Alison.

In this case you could write down:

Ali is on
Ali's son
Al is in
I listen

You now have to think of a way to continue the sentence that makes sense (yes, jokes do have to make sense). Take 'Ali is on'. This could become: 'Ali is on television, can I come in to watch?'

Work with the others in the same way and you have four 'knock, knock' jokes from the one name:

Knock, knock.
Who's there?
Alison.
Alison who?
Ali's on TV, can I come in to watch?

Knock, knock.
Who's there?
Alison.
Alison who?
Ali's son wants to know if his dad's in there.

Knock, knock.
Who's there?
Alison.
Alison who?
Al is in, can I come in, too?

Knock, knock.
Who's there?
Alison.
Alison who?
Alison to my radio every day.

Here are some ideas of how other names can be used:

Ben: Ben-d down . . . Ben away (Been away) . . .
Arthur: Are there . . . ? 'Arf a (Half a) . . .
Joan: Do you own (say it quickly) . . .
Marty: My tea . . . Mighty . . . Martini . . .
Shirley: Surely . . .
Olive: I live . . .
Tamara: Tomorrow . . .
Sonia: It's on your . . . It's only a . . .
Alec: I like . . . I lick . . .
Hugo: You go . . .
Mona: Moaner . . . Mown a . .
Wendy: When the . . .

It is not possible to come up with something for every name but once you start trying you will be amazed at what you can come up with. Here are a few to get you going:

Knock, knock.
Who's there?
Howard.
Howard who?
Howard I know?

Knock, knock.
Who's there?
Ozzie.
Ozzie who?
Ozzie you later, OK?

Knock, knock.
Who's there?
Nana.
Nana who?
Nana your business.

Knock, knock.
Who's there?
Ewan.
Ewan who?
No, just me.

Knock, knock.
Who's there?
Luke.
Luke who?
Luke through the keyhole and you'll see.

Knock, knock.
Who's there?
Beryl.
Beryl who?
Beryl load of monkeys.

47

Knock, knock.
Who's there?
Bella.
Bella who?
Bella no ring, that's why I knocked.

Knock, knock.
Who's there.
Cyril.
Cyril who?
Cyril pleasure to meet you.

Knock, knock.
Who's there?
Ivor.
Ivor who?
Ivor Got.

Knock, knock.
Who's there?
Justin.
Justin who?
Justin time for lunch.

Knock, knock.
Who's there?
Althea.
Althea who?
Althea later.

Knock, knock.
Who's there?
Don.
Don who?
Don just stand there, open the door.

Knock, knock.
Who's there?
Ivan.
Ivan who?
Ivan to come in.

Knock, knock.
Who's there?
Bibi.
Bibi who?'
Bibi C.

Knock, knock.
Who's there?
Della.
Della who?
Della Katessan.

Knock, knock.
Who's there?
Barbara.
Barbara who?
Barbara black sheep, have you any wool . . .?

Knock, knock.
Who's there?
Ken.
Ken who?
Ken I come in?

Find the Answers

The tag line for each of these jokes is just one word. Can you work our what it is and then find out where it is hidden in the grid of letters on page 53?

The words may be written horizontally, vertically or diagonally, so it is quite hard to do. If you find it too difficult, or you are too lazy to have a go, turn to page 123 for the answers.

To give you a start, the answer to the first joke is 'seven' and one of the other answers has been ringed on the grid.

What odd number becomes even when you take away S?

Something that is full of holes but still holds water.

What's a put-up job?

What animal are you when you take a bath?

The greater it is the less it can be seen. What is it?

Our butcher is rather fat, six feet tall and wears size 11 shoes. What does he weigh?

What do cats read?

What do you get if you cross an athlete with a beach?

What type of coffee is like mud?

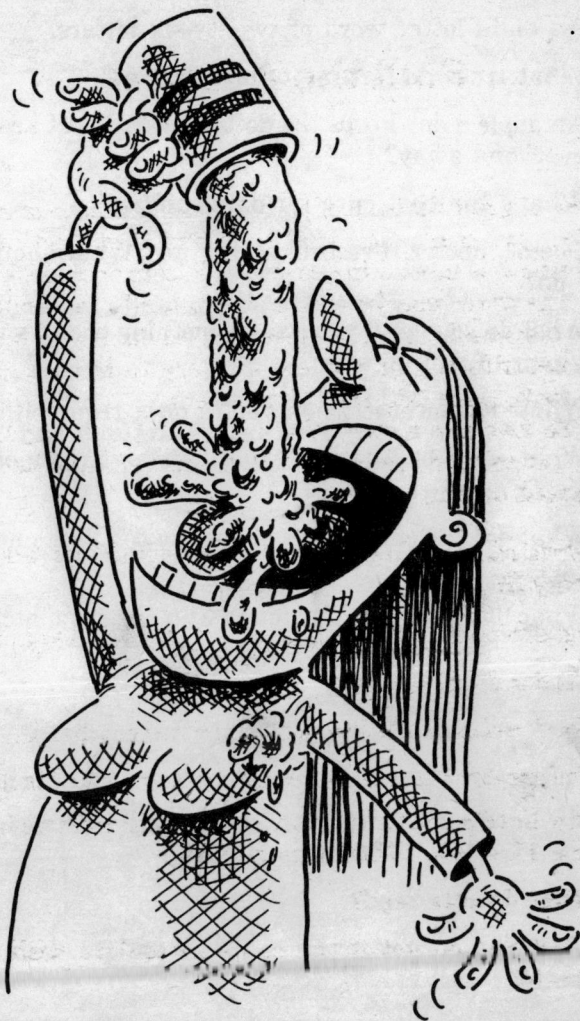

What did the jockey say at the end of the horse race?

An eight-letter word of twenty-six letters.

What trees do fortune tellers look at?

An apple a day keeps the doctor away. What keeps everyone away?

What's the best cure for dandruff?

Doctor, doctor, I've broken my leg. What should I do?

What do you get if you cross something chewy with a pair of wellingtons?

What season is it when you're on a trampoline?

What kind of pliers are used in an arithmetic lesson?

What did the canary say about the cost of its new cage?

What flying creature is found at a cricket match?

```
A B O S D W W H O A L I C B A
D F A P G E A M O L Y B E A R
A S E V E N L I M P R A B T O
M R P S F J L X Z W S L Q R Z
O E Z O X Q P K G Q X D W Z R
G F A T N G A O R V Z N Y S Z
G C X T V G P K O C H E A P L
Y V R A H J E I U C W S X A Z
Z L K L D A R K N E S S B L K
I V R P X Q I G D H Q C R M L
N M Y H C X N B R W U M L S P
E Q O A V B G A R L I C N J H
S H N B B C X W T D C V S Z A
W V R E N M G T W X K V P O R
M U L T I P L I E R S C R X W
X R F G J K H Y G A A C I R Q
C R T G H Y W S K L N D N B Y
G U M B O O T S B V D K G D P
```

Letters of the Alphabet

The answer to each of the following jokes is a letter
of the alphabet. Can you work out they are?
 You will find the answers on page 124.

What letter of the alphabet is . . .

 1 . . . the centre of gravity?
 2 . . . a small vegetable?
 3 . . . a bird?
 4 . . . a hot drink?
 5 . . . an insect?
 6 . . . like an island?
 7 . . . a chicken?
 8 . . . a line of people?
 9 . . . an ocean?
10 . . . a girl's name?
11 . . . a question?
12 . . . the opposite of Heaven?
13 . . . in your head?
14 . . . lazy?
15 . . . the hottest?

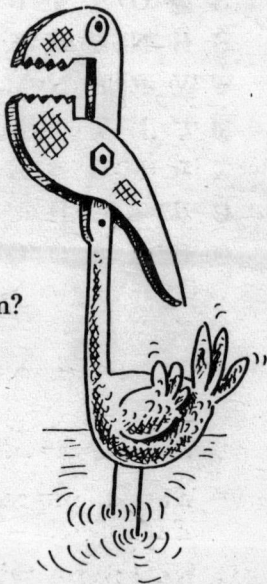

What's in a Name?

The answers to these jokes are all names of people. If you cannot work them out, you will find the answers on page 124.

1 What do you call a man with a rabbit up his jumper?

2 What do you call a man with an insect on his leg?

3 What do you call a girl who has just stood up?

4 What do you call a woman who nags?

5 What do you call a man with ropes hanging from his ears?

6 What do you call a girl with two toilets on her head?

7 What do you call a man with a spade on his head?

8 What do you call a man without a spade on his head?

9 What do you call a man with a wooden head?

10 What do you call a man with eyes in the top of his head?

11 What do you call a man who lives in a narrow street?

12 What do you call a woman who builds bridges?

13 What do you call a man on his knees?

14 What do you call a man who paints?

15 What do you call a barmaid who conjures with the drinks?

16 What do you call a man who wears rings and necklaces?

17 What do you call a man banging at your front door?

18 What do you call a man with a car on his head?

19 What do you call a man with a seagull on his head?

20 What do you call a man wearing ear muffs?

More General Knowledge

See if you can work out the answers to these questions. If you can't, or you prefer to cheat, you will find the answers on page 125.

1 What game did the north wind play with the south wind?

2 What do you call the fleas on a parrot?

3 Who was the youngest newsreader on television?

4 How do you gain the ability to hypnotize people?

5 What is the most shocking city in the world?

6 What's the best material for making kites?

7 What is the untidiest part of an army camp?

8 What British town sells bad meat?

9 What do you call a burning jacket?

10 What do cats try to achieve?

11 What is a polygon?

12 What is copper nitrate?

13 Who won the Black Prince?

14 How do you make a bandstand?

15 What do you call a noisy soccer fan?

Words within Words

If you take an interest in words you will notice that many words have other words in them. Mistletoe, for example has the word 'toe' in it, starboard is made up of 'star' and 'board', chopstick of 'chop' and 'stick', and donkey has the word 'key' in it.

If you speak the words out loud and perhaps change the pronunciation or say them fast you may come up with some other words. Potato, for example, has the word 'toe' at the end. Say potato enough times and you discover that by saying it fast you have potty-toe, and that could be all you need to make a joke. Potty can mean daft so your joke could be:

What is a daft bit of your foot that you have for dinner?

A *potty-toe.*

Let's take mistletoe. Take off the 'toe' (painful) and you are left with 'mistle'. Say this often enough and fast enough and you can make it sound like 'missile'. So:

What do you get if you cross a weapon with a foot at Christmas?

Missile-toe.

For starboard you might come up with:

What plank belongs to a famous actress on a ship?
  Star-board.

All the following jokes use words that contain other words. When you have had a good laugh at them see if you can make up some of your own.

What's the best day for making chips?
  Friday.

What does a chiropodist have for breakfast?
  Cornflakes.

What sort of person makes up jokes about knitting?
  A nitwit.

Why did the Red Indian wear feathers in his hair?
  To keep his wigwam.

What age is most important to a motorist?
  The mileage.

What kind of key has a kick to it?
A donkey.

What do you get if you cross an axe and a stick?
A chopstick.

What type of letters help keep you cool?
Fan mail.

What room has no floor, no door, no windows and no walls?
A mushroom.

What is a fencer's favourite fish?
Swordfish.

What do you call a sleeping child?
A kidnapper.

What do frogs sit on?
Toadstools.

What ship is managed by more than one person?
A partnership.

What do you call a stupid ant?
Ignorant.

What type of pine has the sharpest needles?
Porcupine.

What do baby apes sleep in?
Apricots.

Who is the strongest type of criminal?
A shoplifter.

What is a boxer's favourite drink?
Punch.

What songs are expensive?
For-tunes.

How would you describe an amused herd of cows?
Laughing stock.

More Daft Definitions

All the following words have been defined below in an apt or amusing way. Can you work out which definition belongs to which word?

You'll find the answers (if you need them) on page 125.

1 Free speech. 2 Short cut. 3 Hail. 4 Net. 5 Hermit. 6 Blotting paper. 7 Bachelor. 8 Friend. 9 Coward. 10 Undercover agent. 11 Apology. 12 Conjuring.

a) Holes tied together with string.
b) Hospital for sick cattle.
c) The only thing that enables a man to have the last word in an argument with his wife.
d) Something you search for while the ink dries.
e) A small wound.
f) Using someone else's telephone.
g) A girl's hand.
h) Someone who has the same enemies as yourself.
i) Telling lies with the fingers.
j) Hard-boiled rain.
k) A spy in bed.
l) A man who never has a bride idea.

More Mixed-up Jokes

Here are some jokes where the tag lines have got mixed up. Can you work out which is the correct tag line for each joke? This time there are no answers for you to refer back to. You are on your own!

What box cannot keep a secret?
He wanted to grow mashed potatoes.

Where do they make laws with holes in them?
A jellycopter.

Where would you buy cheese in India?
Gnome work.

What wobbles and flies?
At a Delhi-catessen.

What did the chewing gum say to the carpet?
A scrapbook.

What gets wetter as it dries?
Bolt upright.

How does a robot sit?
The Houses of Polomint.

What do you call a robbery at a fishmonger's?
I'm stuck on you.

Why did the farmer run a steamroller over his field?
A smash and crab raid.

What do elves do after school?
A chatterbox.

What book teaches you how to fight?
A towel.

Doctor, Doctor!

What sort of jokes would you find in a doctor's surgery?

Sick jokes.

The jokes that follow are not exactly sick but some of them may be a little poorly. They are all about doctors, illness or hospital and that is enough reason to put them together in this section. If you *are* sick they are guaranteed to make you feel worse.

Doctor! That's the third operating table you've ruined this week. You must try not to cut so deeply!

Doctor, doctor, I feel like a pair of curtains.

Well, pull yourself together.

Doctor, doctor, I feel like a clock.

Can you wait a tick?

Doctor, doctor, I think I'm invisible.

Who said that?

Why did the nurse tiptoe past the medicine cabinet?

She didn't want to wake the sleeping pills.

Doctor, doctor, I feel like a pack of cards.

I'll deal with you later.

Advice for doctors: In cases of amnesia collect the fee in advance.

My doctor gave me a bottle of pills to improve my strength. There is only one snag — I can't get the lid off.

My doctor said I should bathe in milk to improve my complexion. There's only one snag — I can't get into the bottle.

Doctor, doctor, everyone ignores me.
Next, please!

What's the cure for water on the brain?
A tap on the head.

A man was rushed to hospital with a nasty gash
in his arm. The doctor took one look at it and said,
'Hm, I will have to put a few stitches in that.'

'Thanks, doctor,' said the patient. 'And at the
same time could you sew this button back on my
shirt?'

What did the surgeon say when he accidentally cut
through an artery?
Aorta know better.

An apple a day keeps the doctor away . . . if it's
aimed correctly.

A man telephoned the maternity hospital to see
how his wife was doing. Unfortunately he got
through to the local cricket club by mistake.

'What's the result?' he asked.

He fainted when he heard the reply: 'They're all
out. The last two were ducks . . .'

What's the best way to avoid catching diseases
from biting insects?
Don't bite any insects.

Doctor, are you mad if you talk to yourself?
Only if you answer.

More Letters

There are quite a few words and phrases that sound like several letters of the alphabet strung together. Can you work out which letters provide the answer for each of these jokes. The correct letters are listed on page 125 if you get stuck.

Then see if you can think up some more 'letter' brainteasers.

1 How can you ask for a drink with just three letters?

2 How can you spell 'horse' in two letters?

3 What two letters spell 'jealousy'?

4 What two letters spell 'there is nothing in it'?

5 What four letters could end a game of hide and seek?

6 What letters are never tired?

7 What letters make your teeth bad?

8 What letters can climb up a wall?

9 What letters describe the North Pole?

10 What do you call a Red Indian's tent?

11 What letters make a girl's name?

12 How do you spell 'mousetrap' in three letters?

Did You Hear?

Did you hear about the man who robbed a music shop?
He got away with the lute.

Did you hear about the short-sighted boxer?
He couldn't find the weigh-in.

Did you hear about the bank robber who was so lazy he telephoned the bank and said, 'This is a hold-up. Send me £100,000.'

Did you hear about the couple who met in a revolving door?
They've been going around with each other ever since.

Did you hear about the dog lying in the garden gnawing a bone?
When he got up he found he'd only three legs.

Did you hear about the girl who was so poor she was made in Hong Kong?

Did you hear Gorbachev's latest speech on modernization?
He's going to take the steppes out of Russia and put in escalators.

Did you hear about the man who always wore sunglasses?
He took a dim view of things.

Did you hear about the Japanese millionaire who was asked how he had made his fortune?

He said he had a yen for that sort of thing.

Did you hear about the little boy called Dad?

They named him after his father.

Did you hear about the man who had jelly in one ear and custard in the other?

He was a trifle deaf.

Did you hear about the man who invented a wooden car, with a wooden engine and wooden wheels.

It wooden go.

Did you hear about the cow who had hiccups?
She churned her own butter.

Did you hear about the navvies who went on strike
because a new mechanical shovel was introduced
on the site?
They said it was too dangerous to lean on.

Did you hear about the cross-eyed javelin thrower?
*He never won any medals but he certainly kept
the crowd wide awake.*

Did you hear about the glass blower who inhaled?
Now he's got a pane in his stomach.

Did you hear about the dog who visited a flea
circus?
He stole the show.

Did you hear about the tree doctor who had an
accident?
He fell out of his patient.

Did you hear about the chicken who fell ill?
It got people pox.

Did you hear about the man who died from drinking varnish?

It was a beautiful finish.

Did you hear about the bridegroom who went on honeymoon by himself?

He didn't believe in going out with married women.

Did you hear about the two red blood corpuscles?

They loved in vein.

Did you hear the story about the local dustcart?

It's a load of rubbish.

Did you hear about the woman who uses too much make-up?

Five minutes after she has stopped laughing her face is still smiling.

More Jokes to Fit

The answers to the jokes in this section fit into the grid shown. Can you work out what the answers should be and then fit them into the squares?

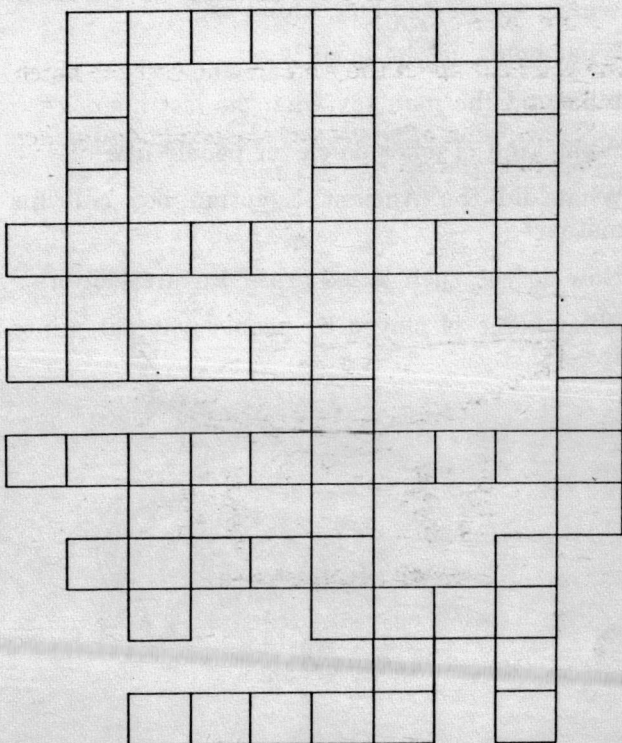

What did the cobbler say when a herd of elephants walked into his shop?

What word is said faster by adding another syllable to it?

What do you make in a hurry?

What do geese eat?

What is the coldest game you can play?

What is a crocodile's favourite game?

What has one eye but cannot see?

What holds up the moon?

What did the man say when he lost his dog?

What kind of jokes do clever people like?

What did the Ancient Egyptian boy call his mother?

How do you spell 'dried grass' in three letters?

What game is played by people who eat minty sweets?

What game is played by six elephants in a telephone box?

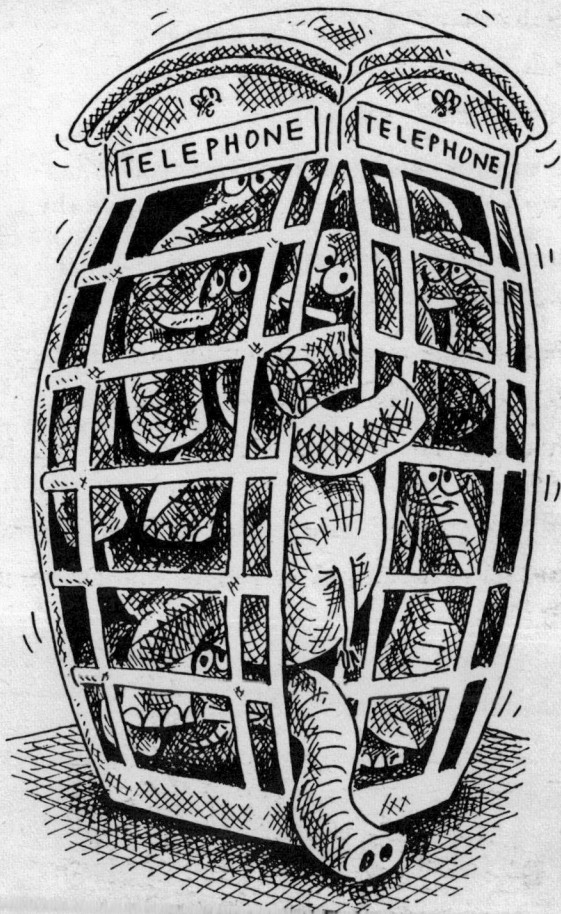

You'll find the finished grid on page 126.

Joke Search

The answer to each of these jokes is just one word and all the answers have been hidden in the grid on page 78. To make the search a little more difficult, the words in the grid are written out horizontally, vertically and diagonally, so you need to work out the answers first.

To give you a start one answer has been ringed, and you may also like to know that one of the answers is 'mittens', but you will have to work out which one.

If you do get stuck turn to page 127 for the answers.

What has four wheels and flies?

If the whole of Ireland was flooded which city would float?

What falls but doesn't get hurt?

Who gets the sack every time he goes to work?

What sort of tiles can't be glued to walls?

How do the Welsh eat cheese?

What invention enables you to see through a brick wall?

What Red Indian tribe had the best lawyers?

What is musical and keeps you dry?

What is brought by the yard and worn by the foot?

What do you get if a cat swallows a ball of wool?

Who hold up trains but are never arrested?

What stays hot in the fridge?

What language is spoken by mathematicians in Cuba?

What do you get if you feed a lemon to a cat?

What wears shoes but has no feet?

What do you call a crazy spaceman?

What kind of song do you sing in a car?

What do you have to be to get a state funeral?

What does a diver get paid if he works extra hours?

```
U D Y P B R I D E S M A I D S
N R U O V T Y M A U V W C Z R
D G H S T H G U L K J O H R A
E W R T T R X S O U R P U S S
R K J M F C X T N K M F M G T
T S W A V U A A B F D T B F R
I C T N F B C R D L O K R F O
M D Y O L I U D T F D S E B N
E W Q K L C V E C G T D L T U
M G W S Q T P L K U Y H L R T
E P C A E R P H I L L Y A R T
N A S W A V G T S W V G H O X
T V X C A R T O O N X Z W U C
M E H F D T I D F D T C O R K
D M G Y U J N G F D S I C A P
X E R V M I T T E N S V T I R
X N A R W V G H J L P I Y N F
C T S D C G T R E P T I L E S
```

Library of Laughs

Great fun can be had by devising your own crazy book titles such as *Lords of the Jungle* by L. E. Fance or *Horse Riding* by Jim Karna.

The easiest way to do this for yourself is to think up the name first. Some words and phrases have a name in them already, such as Penniless (Penny); Frankenstein (Frank); Tomorrow (Tom); Canine (Kay); Antique (Anne).

Another way to come up with a suitable name is to think of a Christian name and then see if you can fit it with a made-up surname. This is rather like devising the 'knock, knock' jokes described on page 44. Some useful names are:

Willie: Will he . . . ? (Will he be good? will he be at home?)

Ivor: I've a . . . (I've a fortune; I've a new one; I forget)

You can also use initials that sound like words such as I.C. (I see; icy) or U.R. (you are).

Once you have got the name, the book title is quite easy to think up. Using the names just mentioned you could come up with the following additions to your library of laughs.

Flat Broke by Penny Less
Make Your Own Monster by Frank N. Stine

It Never Comes by Tom Orrow
It's a Dog's Life by Kay Nine
Old Furniture by Anne Teak
The Naughty Boy by Willie B. Goode
The Student Prince by Willie B. Hansom
Money Isn't Everything by Ivor Fortune
Buying a Car by Ivor Newone
Improving Your Memory by Ivor Gett
Searching for Sheep by I. C. Ewe
The North Pole by I. C. Playce
Stupid People by U. R. Won

Try thinking of names in this way and it will not
be long before you are coming up with some new
book titles to amuse your friends. Here are a few
more to start you off:

How to Make Money by Robin Banks
Calypso Music by Lydia Dustbin
Around the Mountain by Sheila B. Cumming
Cooking on a Barbecue by Sue Pergrub
Blow Up by Dinah Mite
Singing in the Toilet by Hal E. Looya
What's for Breakfast? by Chris P. Bacon
A Cure for Everything by Penny Sillin
She is a Cannibal by Henrietta Mann
Enjoy Your Weekend by Gladys Friday
The Perfect Marriage By Ian Shee
Keep Out! by Doris Closed
Life on The Road by Laurie Driver
How to Draw by Art Master
The Quiet Wedding by Marion Secret
Coping with Noise by Major Headache
Sand in My Shoes by C. Shaw
Gunfight at Dawn by Rick O'Shea
How to Repair Your Car by Mick Anic

Even More General Knowledge

Can you work out the answers to these questions? If you cannot, if you want to cheat, if you are incapable, or if you can't be bothered, you will find the answers on page 127.

1 Who invented spaghetti?

2 What is the Holy See of Rome?

3 What is a down-to-earth story?

4 What's the cheapest time to telephone someone?

5 Who invented fitted carpets?

6 Why do they put telephone wires up so high?

7 Who invented gunpowder?

8 Is it true that married men live longer than single men?

9 How do you join the army?

10 What do pineapple growers do with the pineapples they grow?

11 Why did the man shoot at the clock?

12 Why did the pilot fly upsidedown?

13 What's the quickest way to get your name in the newspaper?

14 What does an astronaut do when he loses his temper?

15 What do you call a flying policeman?

Cats

You may have heard of the musical *Cats*. This page
has got nothing to do with that. But it does have
something to do with cats generally, as you will
see if you keep reading.

The answers to each question are given on page
128. But don't forget that these (like most of the
answers given in this book) are only a guide. As
with any joke, there could be a number of different
replies. So, if you have got something other than
the answer on page 128 do not worry. Your answer
could be funnier or more apt than the one we have
come up with!

1 What cat is wooden?

2 What cat goes around a garden?

3 What cat is one of your family?

4 What cat does your hair?

5 What cat throws stones?

6 What cat is sympathetic?

7 What cat can you put your head on?

8 What cat goes on the stage?

Greetings

How does one angel greet another?
Halo, there!

How does a doctor greet his nurse?
Hi, Jean.

How does one policeman greet another?
Hello, hello, hello.

How does a bee greet a flower?
Hello, honey.

How does orange squash greet a tap?
I'm diluted to meet you.

How does a butcher greet a customer?
Pleased to meet you; meat to please you.

How does a fire greet a hosepipe?
I'm de-lighted meet you.

How does one Hawaiian greet another?
Ha-wa-ya?

How does a detective greet a criminal?
I'm policed to meet you.

How does a doctor greet another doctor?
You're fine, how am I?

How does a gardener greet his hoe?
Hi, hoe.

Daft Definitions Yet Again

Each of the following definitions given below describes one of the words on the following list. Can you work out which definition goes with which word?

There are no prizes for correct answers but if you check your answers with those given on page 128 and you get some of them right you can congratulate yourself for being so clever.

1 Denial. 2 Caterpillar. 3 Bank. 4 Pillow. 5 Monopoly. 6 Rose. 7 Octopus. 8 Meow. 9 Urchin. 10 Knapsack. 11 Cook book.

a) A lonely parrot.

b) Part of a woman's face.

c) A book with a lot of stirring chapters.

d) A place that will lend you money if you can prove you don't need it.

e) An eight-sided cat.

f) A catty remark.

g) An upholstered worm.

h) An Egyptian river.

i) A sleeping bag.

j) Headquarters

k) What a man in a boat does.

Good News, Bad News

GOOD NEWS: We've been given the day off school.
BAD NEWS: We have to go back tomorrow.

GOOD NEWS: Mum's taking me to the zoo tomorrow.
BAD NEWS: She's going to leave me there.

GOOD NEWS: I got a job as a postman.
BAD NEWS: They gave me the sack.

GOOD NEWS: I'm teacher's pet.
BAD NEWS: She keeps me in a cage.

GOOD NEWS: Dad bought a paper shop.
BAD NEWS: It blew away.

GOOD NEWS: My dad got a job as a human cannonball.
BAD NEWS: He's been fired.

GOOD NEWS: I've just invented a cure for amnesia.
BAD NEWS: I've forgotten what it was.

GOOD NEWS: I've been fishing and got lots of bites.
BAD NEWS: They were all from mosquitoes.

A man was lying in hospital after an accident. The surgeon came up to him and said, 'I have some bad news and some good news. The bad news is that I have had to amputate both your legs. The good news is that the man in the next bed wants to buy your slippers.'

GOOD NEWS: I was given a shock-proof, water-proof, anti-magnetic, rust-proof watch for my birthday.
BAD NEWS: It caught fire!

A squadron of soldiers had been on exercise for a week. They were tired, bedraggled and very dirty. The general came up to them and said, 'I have some good news and some bad news. The good news is that you are all going to get a change of clothing. The bad news is that Smith will change with Jones, Brown will change with Baker, Boyle will change with Davies. Green . . .'

More I Wouldn't Say . . .

If you appreciate good insults you can add the ones below to your armoury. Several tag lines are given for each remark but see if you can think up any more (without being too unkind, of course!).

I wouldn't say my brother is unpopular but . . .

. . . no-one telephones him, not even when he's in the bath.
. . . he makes a perfect stranger.
. . . when he tried to borrow 10p to telephone a friend he was offered 20p to call all of them.
. . . he stood under the mistletoe at Christmas and waited for a kiss . . . and he was still there at Easter.

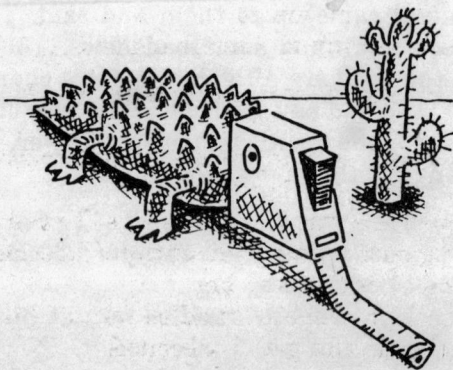

I wouldn't say my girlfriend has got a turned-up nose but . . .

. . . every time she sneezes she blows her hat off.

. . . every time it rains she almost drowns.

. . . when she goes to the zoo people feed her with buns.

. . . she can swim underwater using it as a snorkel.

I wouldn't say Mrs Chatty is a gossip but . . .

. . . when she goes on holiday she spreads sunburn lotion on her tongue.

. . . she was once booked to appear in Aladdin. They wanted to use her mouth for the cave.

. . . she still doesn't know that a telephone is a two-way instrument.

. . . she can always tell you something before you tell her.

. . . she can give you all the details without knowing any of the facts.

. . . she has a good sense of rumour.

I wouldn't say my mother is old but . . .

. . . the candles cost more than her birthday cake.

. . . she's got so many wrinkles on her forehead she has to screw her hat on.

. . . when she was born Billy wasn't even a kid.

. . . she once visited an antique auction and someone tried to buy her.

. . . she has so many candles on her birthday cake the ceiling gets barbecued.

. . . she is approaching middle age for the third
time.

. . . she has got more wrinkles than a pound of
prunes.

. . . by the time the last candle is lit on her birthday cake the first one has gone out.

I wouldn't say my dad was bald but . . .

. . . he combs his hair with a sponge.

. . . it's the first time I've seen a parting with
ears.

. . . he was once mistaken for a honeydew melon.

I wouldn't say Aunty Scrooge is mean but . . .

. . . if she was a ghost she wouldn't even give you
a fright.

. . . every time she changes the water in the
goldfish bowl her husband gets fish soup for his
supper.

. . . if she found a crutch she would break her
husband's leg so she could make use of it.

I wouldn't say Tiny Tim was short but . . .

. . . every time he has toothache he thinks it's
a corn on his foot.

. . . when he pulls up his underpants he blindfolds himself.

. . . he applied for a job in a bank and they told
him to try a piggy bank.

. . . he has to stand on a chair to clean his teeth.

I wouldn't say my friend is tall but . . .

... he was once fined for looking in the windows of low flying aircraft.

... his barber has to use a ladder to cut his hair.

... giraffes look up to him.

I wouldn't say Fred Universe is tough but . . .

   . . . he can eat sardines without opening the tin.
   . . . he uses barbed wire for a hairnet.
   . . . he certainly smells strong.

I wouldn't say my girlfriend is ugly but . . .

   . . . at Christmas her friends hang her up and kiss the mistletoe.
   . . . the day she was born her father went to the zoo and murdered the stork.
   . . . when she sucks a lemon the lemon pulls a face.
   . . . she's got the type of face you don't want to remember but cannot forget.
   . . . she looks like an accident waiting to happen.
   . . . she goes to the beauty parlour on Tuesday and comes back on Friday.
   . . . if beauty is skin deep then she's inside out!
   . . . she rents herself out for Hallowe'en parties.
   . . . she can make yoghurt just by staring at a pint of milk for half an hour.

Just for the Record

Once you start getting into jokes it will not be long before you build up quite a collection. If you are to make any use of this gathering of gags you will have to keep them in some organized way. If you don't, you will not be able to find a joke when you want one and you will also end up with lots of duplicated material.

The easiest way to store all your jokes is on record cards, one card to each joke. These can be kept in a card-filing drawer or a shoe box (take the shoes out first). They can be kept in alphabetical order according to the subject of the joke and new cards can be put in their correct places quite easily.

One snag with the card-filing system is that the cards can prove expensive and they do take up a fair bit of space.

Another solution is to keep them in a loose-leaf binder with a page to each subject. You can get several jokes to a page and new pages are easily added in the right place whenever you want.

But no matter how you keep them you will need some jokes to start off your collection. So the jokes on the following pages have been arranged in alphabetical order under their subject to give you a start.

Even if you do not want to collect jokes you will still find this selection a good giggle.

Angel

Why did the angel lose his job?
He had harp failure.

Antelope

Why do you seldom see an antelope?
Because ants aren't very romantic.

Arab

What do you call an Arab milkman?
A milk sheikh.

Bird

Why did the bird fly over the racecourse?
He wanted to have a flutter on the horses.

Birth

Why were you born in London?
I wanted to be near my mother.

Boomerang

How do you get rid of a boomerang?
Throw it down a one-way street.

Brain

What happened when the idiot had a brain transplant?
The brain rejected him.

Budgerigar

What is the best time to buy budgies?
When they are going cheap.

Buffalo

What's the difference between a buffalo and a bison?
You can't wash your hands in a buffalo.

Cabbage

What do you call two lines of cabbages?
A dual cabbage way.

Calendar

What happened to the man who stole a calendar?
He got twelve months.

Candle

How long does a candle burn?
About one wick.

Car

The latest car has glass floorboards . . . so, when you run over someone, you can see who it was.

Cat

MOTHER: Did you put the cat out?
SON: Why? Is it on fire?

When is it bad luck to have a black cat follow you?
When you are a mouse.

What is the difference between a cat and a comma?
A comma is a pause at the end of a clause while a cat has claws at the ends of its paws.

Cat food

How is cat food sold?
So much purr tin.

Chicken

Why did the farmer make his chickens sit in hot water?
He wanted them to lay hard-boiled eggs.

Child

If a child falls down a well what should you do?
Buy a book on how to bring up children.

Clock

What part of a clock is always old?
The second hand.

Coffee

What happened to the man who didn't know the difference between coffee and petrol?
His car ground to a halt.

Comedian

What does a comedian have for lunch?
Quips with everything.

Cook

Why did the cook have a nervous breakdown?
She couldn't fit round tomatoes into square slices of bread.

Cow

What game do cows like to play?
Moo-sical chairs.

What do you get if you cross a cow with a duck?
Cream quackers.

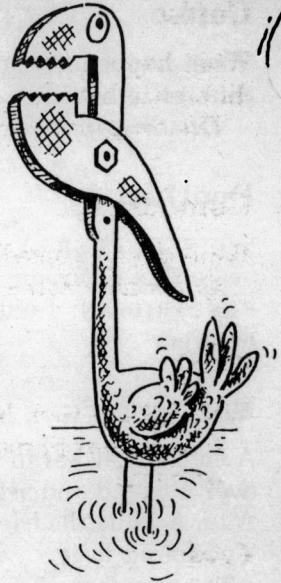

Darling

Is that you, darling?
Yes . . . who's that calling?

Diet

What happens to people who diet?
They have a slim time.

Dog

Why did the Eskimo's dog cough?
He was a little husky.

Dog biscuits

What's the main ingredient in dog biscuits?
Collie flour.

101

Donkey

What did the hungry donkey say when he had only thistles to eat?

Thistle have to do.

Doorbell

HOUSEHOLDER: You were supposed to come yesterday to fix my doorbell.

ELECTRICIAN: I did, sir. I rang twice but got no answer.

Ear

A man lost an ear in an accident at work. He called over a friend and asked him to help search for it. After a while the friend picked up an ear and said, 'I've found it.'

The man looked and said, 'No, that's not the one. Mine had a pencil stuck behind it.'

Egg

What did the egg say to the whisk?

You've beaten me.

Electrician

What did the electrician's wife say when he was late home?

Wire you insulate?

Farmer

Why did the farmer set light to his orchard?

He wanted to grow baked apples.

Fat man

A fat man and an enormous woman have just got
engaged.

They plan to have a big wedding.

What did the fat man say when he ate his dinner?
All that food has gone to waist.

Fight

What would you call a fight between an English-
man and a Japanese?
Punch and judo.

Fire

What is the best way to light a fire with two sticks?
Make sure one of them is a match.

Fish

What two fish are under your foot?
Sole and 'eel.

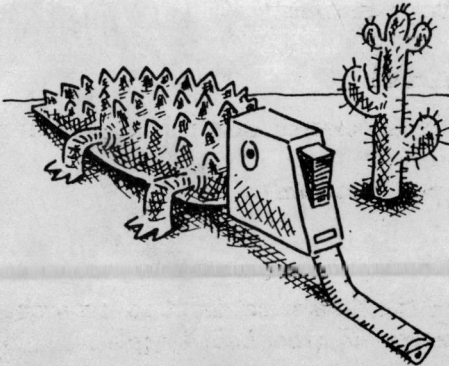

Fisherman

Why did the fisherman put a rubber mouse on the end of his line?

He was trying to catch a catfish.

Flea

How do you find out where a flea has bitten you?
You start from scratch.

How do fleas travel from place to place?
They itch hike.

Fly

Waiter, will you please remove that fly from my plate, I wish to dine alone.

Frog

Why did you put that live frog in your sister's bed?
Because I couldn't find a mouse.

Garden

What smells the most in a garden?
Your nose.

Head

What has a head and a tail but no body?
A coin.

Can you stand on your head?
No, it's too high.

Hedgehog

What did the baby hedgehog say when it backed into a cactus?
Is that you, mother?

Horse

What do you get if you cross a horse with a skunk?
Whinney the Pooh.

What do you give a horse with a cold?
Cough stirrup.

Judge

What did the judge say when he'd finished work?
It's been another trying day.

King Arthur

What was King Arthur's favourite game?
Knights and crosses.

Level crossing

Why was the level crossing gate half open?
The signalman was half expecting a train.

Light bulb

What should you do if you swallow a light bulb?
Use a candle.

Manners

Is it good manners to eat chicken drumsticks with your fingers?
No, you should eat your fingers separately.

Mechanic

Why did the mechanic sleep under the car?
Because he wanted to get up oily in the morning.

Memory

I've got a memory like an elephant.
Yes, and you've got the shape to match.

Metal

Why did the man eat little bits of metal for every meal?
It was his staple diet.

Milk

What has one horn and provides milk?
A milk lorry.

Milking

What happened in the farm when the milking machine broke down?
Udder chaos.

Millionaire

Why did the millionaire have no bathrooms in his house?
Because he was filthy rich.

Mind

I've changed my mind.
Good. Does it work any better than the other one?

Miracle

My dad is a miracle worker. It's a miracle if he works.

Mole

How do you stop moles digging in the garden?
Hide their spade.

What do you get if you cross a mole with a porcupine?
A tunnel that leaks.

Monarch

How would you send a monarch through the post?
By Royal Mail.

Moon

What made the moon turn pale?
At-mos-fear.

Motor cycle

What do you call a motor-cycle thief?
  A *Honda-taker*.

Motorist

Why did the motorist drive everywhere in reverse?
Because he knew the Highway Code backwards.

Music

What sort of music is that?
It's called chamber music.
It sounds as if it's from the torture chamber.

Musicians

What musicians cannot be trusted?
Fiddlers.

Neptune

What would Neptune say if the sea dried up?
I haven't a notion.

North Sea

What is black, hairy and found in the North Sea?
An oil wig.

Octopus

How does an octopus go into battle?
Well armed.

Peas

I eat peas with honey
I've done it all my life.
It may sound kind of funny
— But it keeps them on the knife.

Should you eat peas on an empty stomach?
No, you should eat them on a plate.

Pencil

What did one pencil say to the other?
I've got a leadache.

Peppermint

What is white, lives in the Arctic and tastes of peppermint?
A polo bear.

Politician

What do you get if you cross a politician with a goat?
Someone who is always trying to butt into other people's affairs.

Potatoes

Why did the potatoes argue?
They didn't see eye to eye.

Pub

Why would a pub on the moon be unsuccessful?
It would have no atmosphere.

Quick

What says, 'Quick, quick'?
A duck with hiccups.

Rabbit

What do you call a rich rabbit?
A million-hare.

What did the two rabbits do after they got married?
They went on bunnymoon.

Refrigerator

Why did the boy put his father in the refrigerator?
He fancied an ice-cold pop.

Rent

Why did the woman go into the rent office with a £5 note in each ear?
She was £10 in arrears!

River

What did the river say when the elephant sat in it?
Well, I'm dammed.

Robber

Why did the bank robber take a bath?
He wanted to make a clean getaway.

Russia

What's the cheapest way to get to Russia?
Be born there.

School

At my school the kids are so tough the teachers play truant.

Seville

What are government workers called in Seville?
  Seville servants.

Ship

How would you describe prehistoric ship disasters?
  Tyrannosaurus wrecks.

Skunk

What do you get if you cross a skunk with a boomerang?

A horrible smell you can't get rid of.

Snake

Why did the two boa constrictors get married?

They had a crush on each other.

What do you call a snake carrying a brief case?

A civil serpent.

Soldiers

Why are soldiers like dentists?

Because they do lots of drilling.

Soup

Where would you get explosive soup?

At the Minestrone of Defence.

Steamroller

Why did the man push his friend under a steamroller?

He wanted a flatmate.

Stupid person

How do you make a stupid person laugh on a Monday?

Tell him a joke on Saturday.

Sums

What does sums and bumps into lights?
  A mothematician.

Sword fight

Where would two motorists have a sword fight?
  On a duel carriageway.

Sword swallower

Why was the sword swallower arrested?
  He hiccoughed and stabbed two people.

Tall man

How can you make a tall man short?
  Borrow all his money.

Television

Why will television never replace newspapers?
  You can't wrap up fish and chips in it.

Toupee

How do you like my new toupee?
  It looks super, you can't tell it isn't a wig.

Traffic warden

What did the traffic warden say after booking several motorists?
  I've done a fine day's work.

Train

How can you tell that a train has gone past?
  By the tracks it leaves.

Tramp

A tramp knocked at the door and asked for some food.

  'Didn't I give you some of my apple pie a week ago?' asked the lady.

  'Yes,' said the tramp, 'but I'm all right again now.'

Turkey

Where do turkeys go to when they die?
  To oven.

Vegetable

What is the best vegetable to have with jacket potatoes?
  Button mushrooms.

Water

What is the best way to keep water out of the house?
  Don't pay the water rates!

Weather

What's the weather like?
  I don't know. It's too foggy to see.

Whale

What do you get if you cross a whale with a Belgian cabbage?
Brussel spouts.

Wife

My wife and I were happy for twenty years . . . and then we met.

Wig

When should you take a wig to a psychiatrist?
When it is off its head.

Work

How many people work in your office?
About half of them.

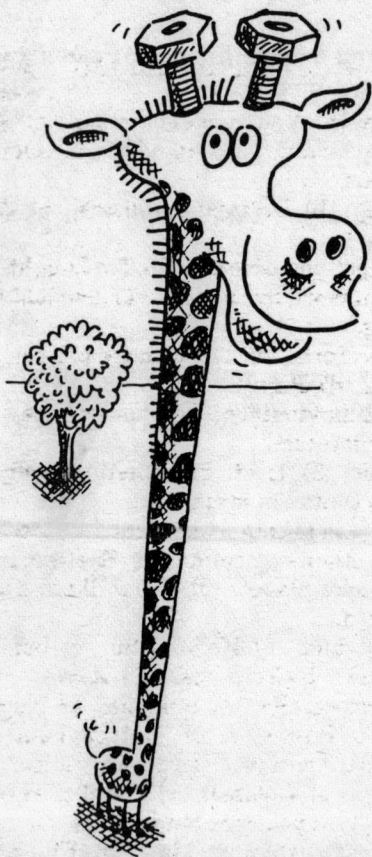

ANSWERS

Finish 'Em Off

1 a) Core! b) You give me the pip. c) When I grow up I want to marry a French Golden Delicious.
2 a) A tap. b) Drainpipe trousers. c) Wear pumps.
3 a) I've got you covered. b) I'm bought by the yard but worn by the foot. c) I've just received a beating.
4 a) Mew York. b) The Canary Islands. c) Cat-mandu. d) Purr-u.
5 a) A duckumentary. b) Quackerjack. c) The feather forecast.
6 a) Panic. b) Try to hit something soft. c) Take a crash course in mechanics.
7 a) She was taking a short cut. b) Because there was no other way round. c) She was trying to get to an udder planet. d) The milkmaid's hands were cold.
8 a) Hiya, bud. b) Hello, petal. c) Leaf me alone.
9 a) Water. b) Your nose. c) A car.
10 a) Nowhere, they sty at home. b) New Pork. c) Porkistan. d) Notting-ham (or any other place with the word 'ham' in it).
11 a) Soup. b) Goldfish. c) Cornflakes (or any other cereal you care to mention).
12 a) It's better than walking. b) They can't afford vacuum cleaners. c) The airlines are on strike.

What Is the Question?

1 What do you get if you cross a dog with a jelly?
2 What is the name of Father Christmas' wife?
3 Why did the man take a pencil to bed?
4 What did the traffic light say to the car?
5 Waiter, this egg is bad.
6 Doctor, doctor, I feel like a window.
7 What do you call a group of road workers falling down a hill?
8 What is a miserable person's favourite pudding?
9 What did the dog say when he sat on a sheet of sandpaper?
10 What is old, pink and wrinkly and belongs to Grandpa?
11 What dance do tin openers do?
12 Are my indicators working?
13 When a man marries how many wives does he get?
14 Why did the burglar cut the legs off his bed?
15 In what type of ball can you carry shopping?
16 What's the difference between Noah's Ark and Joan of Arc?

General Knowledge Quiz

1 On the side of Solomon's head.
2 A scrapbook.
3 A Rolls Rice.
4 Iced lolly.
5 A dwarf in the Paris underground.
6 So their soldiers wouldn't go round the bend.
7 The life story of an automobile.
8 Because they eat light meals.
9 What the pilot says when he bales out.
10 Igloos them together.
11 Sultan Vinegar.

12 Step on his foot outside the church.
13 Justice Thumbs.
14 Use a pair of Caesars.
15 Penicillin.
16 Incorrectly.
17 Streamers.
18 Popcorn.
19 Chessmen.
20 Silence.

Find the Words

Some possible answers:

1 Boiling water.
2 Fly, elephant, cat — whatever you like.
3 Manure or fertiliser.
4 Myth.
5 Porridge, chewing-gum — almost anything gooey
  you can think of.
6 Crocodile, shark — virtually anything that has
  sharp teeth and an appetite.
7 Crocodile, gorilla, almost anything big and
  fearsome.
8 Fire or candle.
9 Pizzas.
10 Ice cream, stick of rock, wound, anything you can
  lick.
11 Lawn mower, spade, any garden implement.
12 Cats and dogs.

Jokes to Fit

	D	R	A	U	G	H	T	S		
	O				O			Q		
	G				O			U		
	G				S			A		
M	O	O	N	B	E	A	M	S		
	N				B			H		
N	E	E	D	L	E				F	
					R				A	
W	I	S	E	C	R	A	C	K	S	
		N			I				T	
	H	A	S	T	E			P		
		P			S	C	H	O	O	L
					A			L		
	M	U	M	M	Y			O		

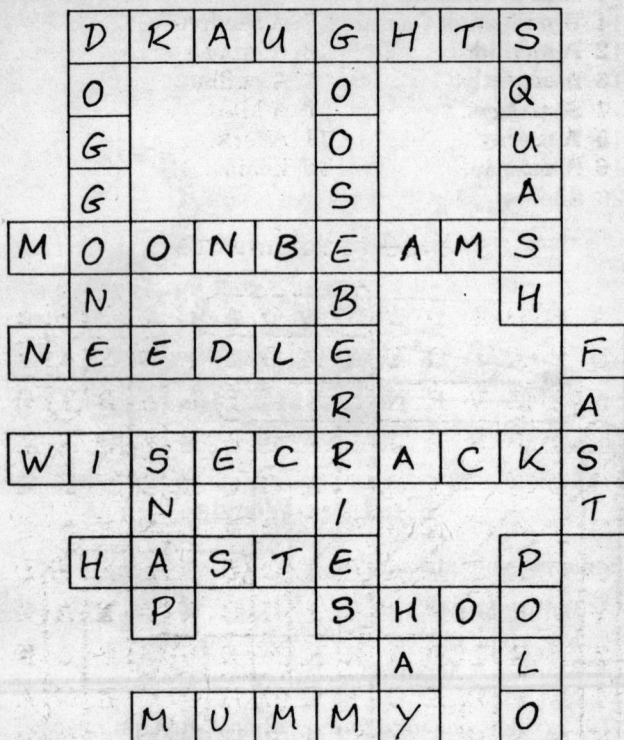

Daft Definitions

1d, 2i, 3g, 4h, 5b, 6l, 7k, 8a, 9c, 10e, 11j, 12f.

Crazy Mixed-up Jokes

1j, 2f, 3g, 4b, 5i, 6h, 7a, 8e, 9d, 10c.

Birds of a Feather

1 A jailbird.
2 A swallow.
3 A crane.
4 A magpie.
5 A turkey.
6 A penguin.

7 A sandpiper.
8 A grouse.
9 A puffin.
10 A kite.
11 A lark.
12 Robin.

Find the Answers

```
A B O S D W W H O A L I C B A
D F A P G E A M O L Y B E A R
A S E V E N L I M P R A B T O
M R P S F J L X Z W S L Q R Z
O E Z O X Q P K G Q X D W Z R
G F A T N G A O R V Z N Y S Z
G C X T V G P K O C H E A P L
Y V R A H J E I U C W S X A Z
Z L K L D A R K N E S S B L K
I V R P X Q I G D H Q C R M L
N M Y H C X N B R W U M L S P
E Q O A V B G A R L I C N J H
S H N B B C X W T D C V S Z A
W V R E N M G T W X K V P O R
M U L T I P L I E R S C R X W
X R F G J K H Y G A A C I R Q
C R T G H Y W S K L N D N B Y
G U M B O O T S B V D K G D P
```

123

Letters of the Alphabet

1 V. 2 P. 3 J. 4 T. 5 B. 6 T – it is surrounded by waTer. 7 N. 8 Q. 9 C. 10 K. 11 Y. 12 L. 13 I. 14 E – because it is always in bEd. 15 B – because it makes oil Boil.

What's in a Name?

1 Warren.
2 Antony (ant on knee).
3 Rose.
4 Mona.
5 Jim (gym).
6 Lulu.
7 Doug.
8 Douglas (Doug-less).
9 Edward.
10 Isiah.
11 Ali.
12 Bridget.
13 Neil.
14 Art.
15 Beatrix (beer-tricks).

16 Jules.
17 Enoch.
18 Jack.
19 Cliff.
20 Anything you like – he can't hear you.

More General Knowledge

1 Draughts.
2 Politics.
3 The one who read the News at Ten.
4 You have a trance-plant.
5 Electri-city.
6 Flypaper.
7 The officer's mess.
8 Oldham.
9 A blazer.
10 Purr-fection.
11 An empty parrot cage.
12 Wages for a policeman's night shift.
13 The son of Old King Cole.
14 Take all their chairs away.
15 A foot-bawler.

More Daft Definitions

1f, 2e, 3j, 4a, 5g, 6d, 7l, 8h, 9b, 10k, 11c, 12i.

More Letters

1 N.E.T. 2 G.G. 3 N.V. 4 M.T. 5 O.I.C.U. 6 N.R.G.
7 D.K. 8 I.V. 9 I.C. 10 T.P. 11 L.N. (and I.V.).
12 C.A.T.

More Jokes to Fit

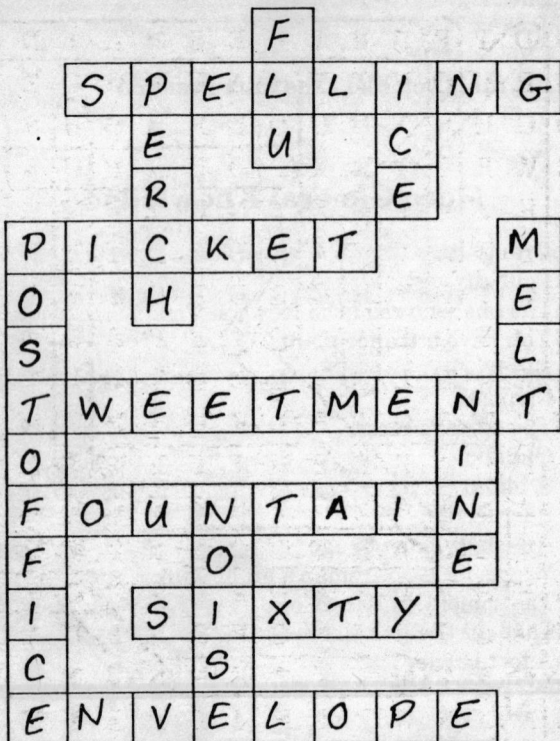

Crossword grid:
- F L U E C E (vertical: FLUENCE)
- S P E L L I N G
- P E R (POST... SPELLING cross)
- P I C K E T
- I C H
- M E L T (vertical: MELT)
- P O S T O F F I C E (vertical)
- T W E E T M E N T
- I N
- F O U N T A I N E (vertical TAINE)
- N O
- S I X T Y
- S I S
- E N V E L O P E

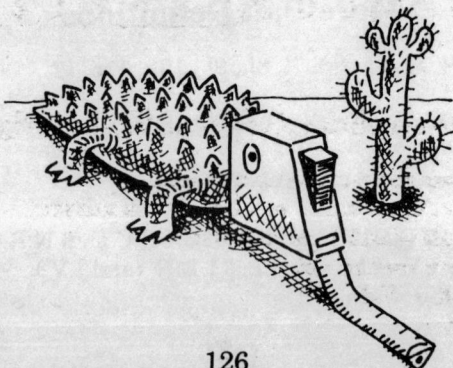

126

Joke Search

```
U D Y P B R I D E S M A I D S
N R U O V T Y M A U V W C Z R
D G H S T H G U L K J O H R A
E W R T T R X S O U R P U S S
R K J M F C X T N K M F M G T
T S W A V U A A B F D T B F R
I C T N F B C R D L O K R F O
M D Y O L I U D T F D S E B N
E W Q K L C V E C G T D L T U
M G W S Q T P L K U Y H L R T
E P C A E R P H I L L Y A R T
N A S W A V G T S W V G H O X
T V X C A R T O O N X Z W U C
M E H F D T I D F D T C O R K
D M G Y U J N G F D S I C A P
X E R V M I T T E N S V T I R
X N A R W V G H J L P I Y N F
C T S D C G T R E P T I L E S
```

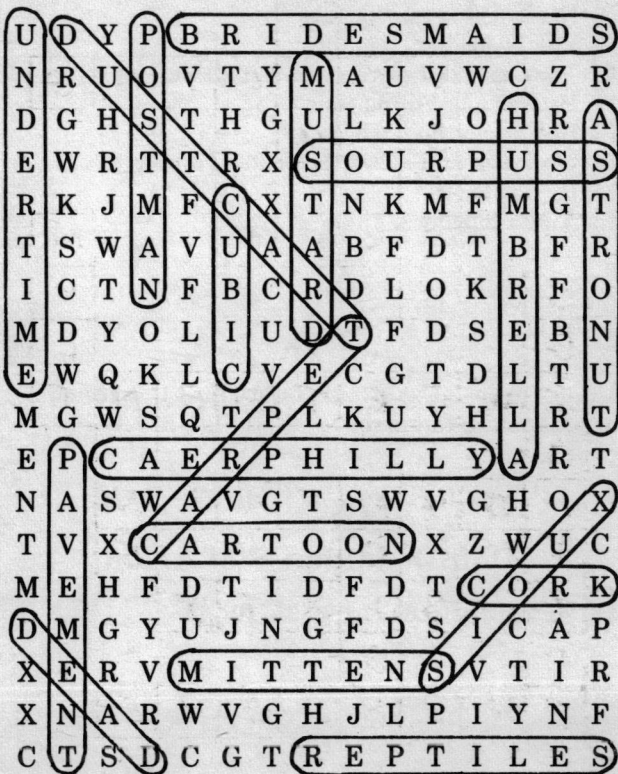

Even More General Knowledge

1 Someone who used his noodle.
2 The Pope looking at himself in a mirror.
3 A tale about a parachutist.
4 When they're out.
5 Walter Wall.

6 To keep up the conversation.
7 A woman who thought guns should look pretty.
8 No, it just seems longer.
9 Tie the soldiers together.
10 They eat all they can and can all they can't.
11 He was just killing time.
12 He'd forgotten his braces.
13 Walk across a busy road reading one.
14 He blasts off.
15 A heli-copper.

Cats

1 Cat-alogue. 2 Cat-awaul. 3 Cat-kin. 4 Cat-acomb.
5 Cat-apult. 6 Cat-arrh. 7 Cat-erpillar. 8 Cat-aract.

Daft Definitions Yet Again

1h, 2g, 3d, 4j, 5a, 6k, 7e, 8f, 9b, 10i, 11c.